S0-ACX-588

THE DEPTHVALE DETECTIVES

and the great

EDUCATION CRISIS

WHAT PEOPLE ARE SAYING

"Don't let the story format fool you—this is a deep dive into school culture and practices. *The Depthvale Detectives* provides an opportunity for teams and individuals to engage in thinking, dialogue, growing, and change without accusations or judgment of how your school has operated in the past. . . . I look forward to sharing this book and engaging teams in new ways. We can all identify the 'crises' in our systems. Now, let's engage and learn so that we contribute back!"

— **Ellen Perconti**
Superintendent
Goldendale School District, United States

"When learning is student centered, equitable, and purposeful, everyone benefits. . . . If you are a teacher or administrator and are not sure how to begin to create meaningful change, this book is a great place to start."

— **Enid Smith Becker**
National Board Certification Secondary Teacher
International School, United States

"Contributive learning is the only counter to an environment of crisis—a powerful and succinct message conveyed through an illustrative and engaging story that cuts across complexity and makes the idea come alive."

— **Vishal Talreja**
Cofounder
Dream a Dream, India

"This book is what we need today! . . . The concept of contributive learning is very powerful and speaks to the need to see beyond the immediacy of our typical metrics. We all need to be in learning for the long run. As I read the book, I envisioned a community-read approach with discussion among and across different groups—students, teachers, families, youth organizations. . . . This book is a resource to drive change."

— **Catherine Millett**
Educational Testing Service (ETS), United States

"I have really enjoyed reading and learning from this book. . . . What if we saw our learners as capable, curious, and full of potential, and that perhaps our current system does not reveal all that potential? What if we led an inquiry into creating opportunities for our learners and educators to make a difference in their world? To see contributive learning as an ESSENTIAL outcome of educational systems would be a bold and exciting move in the right direction."

— **Dr. Jean Clinton**
Clinical Professor
Department of Psychiatry and Behavioral Neurosciences,
McMaster University, Canada

"Educators' bookshelves and inboxes are full of articles, books, and emails about how education needs to change, how to lead change, the importance of school culture, and on and on. But many of these books are abstract and clinical—what is ultimately missed is the connection. *The Depthvale Detectives* uses the power of storytelling to connect readers to the change that is essential in education. Every educator will be able to read this, see themselves and their school, and begin to think about how they can truly contribute to their own school community."

— **Patrick Fisher**
Principal
Meramec Elementary, United States

"The crisis is here. And really, it has always been here. . . . The question now is: What can be done? When will we stop to take the deliberate, creative action needed to combat the crisis? My hope is now. If we do, then we will have moved this tale from story to reality—and, in doing so, made a better world."

— **Dr. Chris Unger**
Teaching Professor
Graduate School of Education, Northeastern University, United States

"This guidebook reminds educators to lean into opportunities that create connections for students and staff. . . . I would recommend this exploratory process for any educator seeking a renewed vision for teaching and learning."

— **Judy A. Fancher, Ed.D.**
Assistant Superintendent, Curriculum and Instruction
United States

"I found the way the story takes the concept of change management and change agents and brings them to life to be invaluable. . . . *The Depthvale Detectives* will help us move to a more inclusive school focused on well-being, meaning, and fulfillment."

— **Chris Dench**
Principal
Kilcoy State High School, Australia

"As a teacher, it is so essential not to get so lost in our work (curriculum, standards, and assessments) that the purpose is lost. It is time to take a look at the big picture. . . . This book gives contributive learning the imagination required to engage readers and at the same time present the material we need. Fantastic!"

— **Suzanne Lewis**
Teacher
Holy Rosary School, United States

"Innovative and timely. *The Depthvale Detectives* takes a substantively different approach to 'How to Improve Schools,' both in terms of content and format. . . . The end result is students and staff who can contribute to making this world a better place."

— **Dr. Jennifer Adams**
CEO
Educating Leaders Consulting, Canada
Executive Committee Member
Karanga: The Global Alliance for Social Emotional Learning and Life Skills

"With great diversity of characters and a student-led focus, this book teaches young people that they do not need to wait for someone else to start something, that they have the ability and power to make change in their communities in many different ways if they just start somewhere."

— **Vipin Thekk**
Director, Youth Years
Ashoka, United States

"The story of the Depthvale Detectives is gripping. I could not stop reading once I started. When overlaid with the exercises and reflections that are included for the 'Change Team,' the book transcends all boundaries and becomes relevant to everyone who interacts with the education system—including students, teachers, school leaders, administrators, parents, and even the media."

— **Suchetha Bhat**
CEO
Dream a Dream, India

"In *The Depthvale Detectives*, ordinary people become heroes in a story that empowers change at the grassroots of our schools—our classrooms. It exposes the barriers faced by leaders, teachers and students as they tackle some of our biggest issues, and serves as a 'how-to' manual for focusing on what really matters in education. . . . The issues facing our schools, communities, and world seem overwhelming. But this book shows us that, together, we can overcome them."

— **Mary Coverdale**
Director
The Learner First, Australia

"*The Depthvale Detectives and the Great Education Crisis* is a fantastic resource for schools. . . . The purpose of school and education ought to be to make people's lives and the world better. Contributive learning is a brilliant way of thinking about how to realize that purpose, how to add to the world."

— **Dominic Regester**
Program Director
Salzburg Global Seminar, Austria
Executive Committee Member
Karanga: The Global Alliance for Social Emotional Learning and Life Skills

THE DEPTHVALE DETECTIVES

and the great

EDUCATION CRISIS

A Guide to Contributive Learning in Schools

by

Joanne McEachen *and* **Matthew Kane**

with illustrations by Natalie Baron

Copyright © 2020 by The Learner First

Foreword copyright © 2020 by Marc Brackett

All rights reserved. No part of this book may be reproduced in any form or by any electronic or mechanical means, including information storage and retrieval systems, without permission in writing from the authors, except by reviewers, who may quote brief passages in a review.

www.depthvaledetectives.com

ISBN-13: 978-0-578-73174-2

Library of Congress Control Number: 2020914933

The characters, places, and events in this book are fictitious. Any similarity to real persons, living or dead, is coincidental and not intended by the authors.

Illustrations by Natalie Baron.
Book design by Trudy Lane.

First Edition: August 2020
Also available as an ebook.

Published by The Learner First
Seattle, Washington, USA
info@thelearnerfirst.com

FOREWORD

By Marc Brackett, Ph.D.

Director, Yale Center for Emotional Intelligence

Professor, Yale Child Study Center

Author of *Permission to Feel*

Emotion scientists are curious and inquisitive. They're connected to the feelings of others around them, and they seek out the stories behind people's behaviors to better understand what's happening and why. Listening, of course, is just the first step—what we do with the stories we hear makes the difference.

With *The Depthvale Detectives and the Great Education Crisis*, Joanne McEachen and Matthew Kane share the much-needed story of contributive learning in a way that helps educators, parents, and students understand, and stand up to, the crisis on our hands.

If you think that a narrative with fictional characters won't give you the tools to make change in your school, you'll be surprised by what you find in the pages that follow. Like with a lot of our feelings and behaviors, there's more to this story than first meets the eye. Its memorable characters and wonderful narrative, and the embedded five phases of the Change Team Experience, will help close the gap between where you are now and where you'd really like to be as a school—and a person.

At the Yale Center for Emotional Intelligence, we talk about closing this gap with the "meta-moment," a pause to consider what your *best self* would do in that specific situation or moment of time. This book marks a true meta-moment for schools, a chance to consider what your *best school* would look like, and to choose the behaviors that bring it to life.

Try to approach it like a scientist—or, detective—pausing to consider what's happening, why, and ways forward in your classroom, school, or community. How are you feeling? Where are you now? What needs to change? And how can you do it? Your best is never more than a moment away.

The best schools help kids close the gap to their best selves. And *The Depthvale Detectives* can help anyone get there.

It gives educators, students, parents—everyone—wholehearted permission to add to the world.

THE DEPTHVALE DETECTIVES

and the great

EDUCATION CRISIS

WELCOME

Wherever you are, whatever your curriculum, whomever you're teaching, our promise is this: all of your students can learn to contribute, to add to the world in all manner of ways. When they do, then no matter their plans or pursuits, they'll have what they need to find real success. Because the very best outcome we can hope for—from anything—is to make people's lives, and the world, better.

Too often, in the course of their academic learning, students aren't getting what they need to succeed. That's what we mean by the Great Education Crisis. No wealth of knowledge, distinctions, or pathways can guarantee meaning, fulfillment, or well-being. We still have to choose the *right* path in our lifetimes, one where our actions improve people's lives, where we use all our "powers"— our learning—for good.

The path to success is **contributive learning**, our term for learning to add to the world. In schools, no aim could be greater than that. But what does it look like . . . and how can you get there?

The story that follows can help guide your way. You may choose to read it with others in your school, as a "Change Team" of educators learning together. Or you may choose to read it outside a school context, finding in the story, its town, and its characters connections that add in other ways to your life. In all cases, when you come to the breaks in the story (one for each phase of the Change Team Experience), we hope you'll take time to reflect on your journey, to identify goals for your school or community, and to come up with steps to achieve them together. Your work will make lives and communities better. And nothing could ever be better than that.

There are so many ways we can add to the world. Which is why, in an equitable, purposeful environment, students succeed when they learn to contribute—and do, in their own individual way. That, we believe, is the way it should be.

Because, after all, we are what we add.

DARK DAYS IN DEPTHVALE

Not far away, in a long emerald valley, a river wound out from the woods into Depthvale.

The people who lived there were charmed by the town, with its tangle of storefronts, streetlights, and houses that stretched from each bank of the river to hillside. "You could wander the world for the rest of your life without finding it anywhere else," they would say.

But lately, for many who called the town home, "anywhere else" had a stronger appeal. Because nothing, it seemed, had gone Depthvale's way.

From a recent health crisis and an economic downturn to violence, unrest, and other challenges locally, the town was already in over its head—and the tide didn't show any signs of receding.

The result was a darkening cloud over Depthvale. If all its inhabitants' thoughts and expressions were combined to give one single face to the town, there's one thing its features would have told you for certain:

The people of Depthvale were down on their luck.

Along with their parents and the other adults, the kids had a lot to be down about, too. They felt that some powerful, invisible force had moved over Depthvale and into their homes. And even though they didn't know exactly what it was, they knew it wasn't good. And a lot of them were scared.

The kids' fears were felt all throughout the community, and nowhere as much as in Depthvale's schools. The weight of what students were bringing to the classroom was like nothing their teachers had experienced before. And the teachers, too, had concerns of their own. Especially those stuck in struggling schools. . . .

One of those schools was Clover K-8 School.

If Depthvale's luck had been lousy of late, then Clover's in years past was downright disastrous. And the town's recent troubles only made matters worse. Declining enrollment, below-average test scores, and now, a district that had to cut costs. . . . It all tallied up to an uncertain future, and it made the experience of being in school less rewarding for students and professionals alike.

They knew in their hearts what they wanted for kids, and the staff felt prevented from making it happen. In turn, a crippling, harsh moral dissonance constantly gnawed at their sense of well-being.

✳ ✳ ✳

With a mysterious shadow hanging over their heads, the K-8 students at Clover responded like anyone would in their shoes. Some acted out in disruptive ways, others hid troubling feelings inside, and all had their focus occasionally interrupted by thoughts unrelated to school.

And Ms. Monica's students weren't any exception. Had strangers been dropped in the walls of her classroom, they might have thought, "Some of these students are hopeless!"

But Ms. Monica wasn't a stranger to her students. She cared about all that went on in their lives, and she tried to support them however she could.

As a result, they worried her sick. And more so with each passing day. . . .

One afternoon, after carefully searching her students' expressions and sensing the melancholy mood in the classroom, Ms. Monica's voice quivered softly mid-sentence and broke off before she could finish.

"Class . . ." she started again after pausing, "whatever you're going through, I'll always be here for you."

Her students moved up a little higher in their seats.

"I know that these last couple months have been tough, but we have what it takes to get through this together. You all mean so much to me," she said, smiling softly. "We may be down now . . . but we'll lift one another."

Ms. Monica's words added warmth to the room. And they made the most lasting impression on Kaia.

Above all, that's because Kaia was connected. She saw and admired the best things in everyone and jumped to add more to their lives where she could. In turn, she felt close to her classmates, her family, and everyone else who she met on her way. She listened to things that were said and unspoken, and she learned from whatever she heard.

You might think that others saw Kaia as a try-hard—a teacher's pet, even. But nobody did. Rather than setting her apart from her classmates, her qualities drew Kaia into their lives. So, like their teacher, she knew they were struggling.

Lying on her living room floor late that night with an ear to the news coming through the TV, Kaia turned thought after thought in her head.

Her personal experiences and what she saw in the news provided countless examples of wrongs in the world, and of people who struggled to do what was right. Environmental, health, and humanitarian crises . . . personal hardships . . . violence in schools. . . .

"What's going on? . . ." Kaia wondered aloud.

But she remembered Ms. Monica's call to the class. "I *know* that we have what it takes," she determined.

And from what she could tell, there was no time to waste.

THE CHANGE TEAM EXPERIENCE

WELCOME, CHANGE TEAM

Change isn't easy—but it's easier together.

Change Teams bring teachers, school leaders, and other school staff *together* to work toward contributive learning. They come up with ways to put well-being first, and to help students learn how to add to the world.

Your school may have something like a Change Team already, or a small group of people who'd be willing to form one. If so, you're in luck—these breaks in the story are written for Change Teams, to help you reflect on the story and its characters and bring change to life for your students.

If not, or if you don't work in a school, it's still an experience worth having. Try to reflect individually, to learn from the process, and, when you can, to share your learning with others.

By the end of the story, and of these first five phases of the Change Team Experience, we hope you'll be ready to commit to contribution. But, for now, *start with yourselves*.

PHASE 1: START WITH YOURSELVES
Who are we, really?

In order to work most effectively together, it's important to know who you each really *are*. You may already know the others on your Change Team well. Or, you may not know much about them at all. Either way, there's more left to learn—and all of it matters.

Here and always, keep the **Four Pillars of the Change Team** in mind.

HONESTY	Say what you really believe.
OPENNESS	Open yourselves up to others.
MINDFULNESS	Be present, attentive, and kind.
BELONGING	Give everyone permission to add.

STEP 1. Who are YOU?

Reflect on this question individually. What are your interests, hobbies, and goals? What's your personal story? What makes you "you"? Then, one at a time, share with your team. After a teammate shares, take time for questions and for others to share what you heard, learned, and value in your teammate.

STEP 2. Who are you as a SCHOOL?

Reflect individually, then share as a team. Focus on culture, mentality, and identity. What's it like to work there? To be a student? A parent? Build a common understanding of your school in **reality**.

STEP 3. Who are you as a COMMUNITY?

Reflect individually, then share as a team, drawing from the prompts in Step 2 above. Describe your community and where your school fits in.

* ACTION. *

Carry honesty, openness, mindfulness, and belonging out into the world and to others around you. Open your eyes to your students, your colleagues, the state of your school, and your own ways of being—see them for all that they are and can be.

A CRISIS OF CONNECTION

By the closing bell's ring on the following school day, Kaia didn't feel any closer to an answer. In fact, she felt even further away.

Recent events made school harder for some. But when it came to assignments, projects, and tests, some of her classmates had always had trouble. And it wasn't just schoolwork that kept students down. Kaia's friends struggled with other things, too. And regardless of how well they did in their classes, a lot of them didn't like being at school. . . .

"How can I get to the bottom of this?" Kaia mused on her short walk from Clover.

With more questions than answers, she entered her house.

Right away, Kaia sensed something was off. She saw her mom, Jasmine, in her office as usual, with a headband that peeked through her long, dark hair. But without Jasmine's usual back-from-school greeting, her chair swiveled quietly around to face Kaia.

Jasmine was an artist. She painted and sketched, sculpted, and ran a small graphic design firm. Her artwork was constantly taking new shapes, and Kaia loved watching it all come to life.

Jasmine's connection with Kaia was special. They gathered a lot without needing to ask. And so, looking up at her mom, Kaia waited.

"Your dad left the network today," Jasmine said.

"Oh . . . that's good," Kaia answered. But she frowned.

Her dad, Wallace, worked at Channel 9 News, and she knew that he'd struggled in his role for a while. As he liked to tell Kaia and her older brother, Cameron, its opinions were often misaligned with his own.

But Kaia and Jasmine both wondered, *"What now? . . ."*

When Kaia heard Wallace and Cameron walk in, she ran to her dad and threw her arms around his waist.

"I'm guessing you heard?" Wallace asked. Kaia nodded. "But maybe you didn't hear *how* it went down? . . ."

Kaia shook her head "no," and then started to smile.

"Well, I stormed out of a meeting and up to the rooftop and shouted at the top of my lungs, '*I QUIT!*' Then I took off my glasses, tied on my cape, and flew off to fight crime in Depthvale!"

"Our very own superman," Jasmine kidded in reply, while Kaia, still picturing the scene in her head, melted in sidesplitting laughter.

"Was it hard for you to quit, Dad?" she asked.

Wallace sighed. "In some ways, it really does hurt to be leaving. A lot has been happening in Depthvale lately. But at Channel 9 News . . . I wasn't much help. And worse, I felt like a part of the problem. We sure didn't offer any real solutions."

Frowning slightly, he added, "But it's a little unsettling. Now that I've left, I'm not sure what I'll do."

Standing next to Kaia, Cameron nodded knowingly. Uncertain of his interests for a career or future study since he graduated high school the previous spring, he'd been working a part-time position in town renting video equipment at a friend's family shop.

"I know what you mean, Dad," Cameron began. "High school was easy, but since then . . . now what? School never gave me the answer to that."

Kaia watched Wallace's eyes fill with worry. She knew Cameron's struggles weighed heavily on her parents, and Kaia was feeling the weight of them, too.

"At least now," Wallace said, putting a hand on Cameron's shoulder, "we can both try to work out our futures together."

Later that night, with news headlines, her family, and her classmates in her head, and feeling more than ever like the Depthvale community was stuck in the shadow of some invisible foe, Kaia went looking for help.

"Dad . . ." she began, "can I ask you a favor?"

Wallace muted the volume on Channel 9 News. "Much better," he winked, adding softly, "what's up?"

"My class has been having a pretty hard time lately," Kaia said slowly. She shuffled in place. "I know you don't work at the network anymore . . . but you still know so much about everything that's happening. I think you could help make us all feel better."

While listening, Wallace watched Kaia affectionately. "It would be my great honor," he said with a smile. "If you think I can help, name the time and I'm there."

She kissed her dad's cheek, and then ran off to bed.

Kaia spoke with her teacher the very next day. And the day after that, as the class shuffled in, Ms. Monica thanked their guest speaker for coming.

"It's my pleasure," Wallace said, looking over the room. "It's nice to be back in a classroom again. I was a teacher myself way back when. . . ."

Once the class settled in, Wallace went to the whiteboard. He wrote the word "CRISIS" in big, capital letters.

"This word has popped up quite a bit lately, hasn't it?" said Wallace, and the class slowly nodded in agreement. "We hear about 'crises' on the news, or from others, and we feel their effects. But what *is* a crisis?"

The class listened silently, and Wallace continued. "A crisis subtracts from our lives and the world. They come in all shapes—as problems, or hardships, or wrongs done to us, or wrongs we do to others. . . . Some burden everyone, others just Depthvale, and some only one or a few of us experience. They make our lives hard. And they can't go ignored."

Sharing with the students about a few public crises, Wallace explored what was happening and why. He talked about his old job at Channel 9 News and explained what it's like to report on big issues.

"Too often," Wallace said, as he stepped toward the students, "people get pushed to the side of these stories. Agendas and biases get in the way, and we forget—or don't care—about the lives that are affected.

"It seems that with a lot of the problems of the day, the underlying thread is a *crisis of connection*. Wherever we're numb to the well-being of others . . . you can bet without question that crisis is king."

The students looked thoughtfully up at the speaker. When Ms. Monica asked them, "Any last questions?" Kaia's friend Jamie put her hand in the air.

"Is there anything we can do to get us out of this mess?" she asked.

Wallace laughed. "I'm glad that you asked! I know it might seem like a problem's too big, or that others are better positioned to solve it. But we *all* can contribute, and all problems have solutions." He smiled. "We just have to find them."

In parting, he added, "Always remember . . . a little connection can go a long way."

The students applauded and Wallace waved goodbye, giving Kaia a quick hug on his way out the door.

"How was I?" he whispered.

"You're amazing," she beamed back.

Though they still felt the lingering burden of crisis, the students were happy to finally learn more—and also to hear there might be a way out.

WHEN WILL WE EVER USE THIS?

When Wallace departed, they got back to their schoolwork.

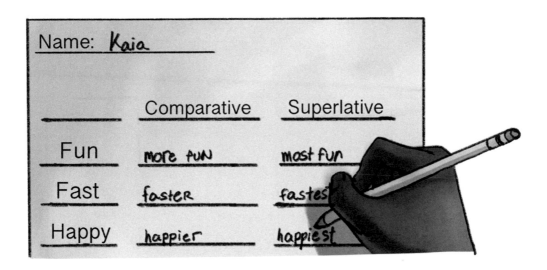

And after the language arts period ended, while listening to another of Ms. Monica's lessons a student put his hand in the air.

"Yes, Lucas?" said Ms. Monica warmly.

His voice came out slowly, and soft as a whisper. "When will we ever *use* this?" he asked.

Ms. Monica's heart sank. She wished that she knew.

"I'm sorry, Lucas . . ." she answered sincerely. Then she added, less confidently, "It might come in handy."

Lucas was gracious enough to agree. But Ms. Monica knew how he felt all the same. She remembered once asking that very same question—and never receiving an adequate answer.

Thoughtfully, Kaia glanced over at Lucas. They'd partnered on a lot of assignments that year, and she knew that he struggled with most of his schoolwork.

But, on the other hand, Jamie did not—Kaia hadn't ever seen her struggle with a lesson. But she also never saw her get excited in the classroom. For Jamie, it was easy—but never enjoyable. Which is why Kaia noticed, after Lucas's question, that Jamie perked up in her seat just a little . . . only to sink down again with the answer.

"What's on their minds? . . ." Kaia thought to herself. She made it a point to find out.

At recess, Kaia saw Lucas on the playground, sitting on the grass with his back to a tree trunk. Since he started at Clover at the beginning of the year, Kaia had seen Lucas sitting there often.

Standing over Lucas was Dylan—a classmate, and one who'd been known to get into some trouble. If a classroom misconduct was in need of a culprit, people were quick to point fingers at him.

Whenever she could, Kaia reached out to Dylan. But she couldn't help feeling that she never got through to him. As far as she knew, nobody had. Kaia wasn't sure that he had any friends, or even anybody to talk to. Mostly, he acted like Kaia wasn't there. Which is better than could be said for a lot of her classmates. . . .

Dylan said something to Lucas, sneered, and then walked to the opposite end of the playground where, every day, he played tetherball alone.

Kaia walked over to Lucas's tree. "Thanks for being my partner in language arts class," she said. "That worksheet was probably the *funnest* of the year."

Of all Lucas's classmates, he was least shy with Kaia. Still, he flushed when he saw her, and smiled.

"What's that?" Kaia asked. She pointed to a notebook lying open in his lap.

After hesitating for a moment, he replied, "They're my stories."

Seeing Kaia's curiosity, he handed over the notebook.

Kaia was blown away. She flipped through the pages, story after story, complete with all sorts of imaginative illustrations.

"These are amazing . . ." she began. Then she stopped.

Reaching the end of the series of stories, Kaia turned the notebook around to face Lucas.

"Your dad gave me the idea," Lucas said, looking up. "Crises are scary, but we can get through them. And maybe . . ." he muttered, "this story will help."

"I *know* it will help," Kaia said back in wonder.

Recently, Kaia overheard a conversation her parents were having about Lucas's mom. She had just lost her job, and they might have to move again.

"Your mom must love reading your stories," Kaia said.

"She might . . ." Lucas answered. He looked at the ground. "But she wants me to get better grades most of all."

Kaia understood. Until moments before, his notebook had always stayed closed to the world.

She sat down beside him with her back to the tree trunk and read through his stories until the bell rang them in.

CONNECTING THE DOTS

When the bell rang again and she left for the weekend, Kaia collected her thoughts.

She remembered the question Lucas posed to Ms. Monica: "When will we ever *use* this?"

Before that day, Kaia had no idea about Lucas's creativity—and every idea about his struggles in school. She also knew Lucas wasn't one to complain. Whatever they worked on, Lucas worked hard. And the class they were in when he asked, Kaia realized, was actually Lucas's favorite.

"It isn't that Lucas didn't care . . ." Kaia thought. "He wanted to learn—and he wanted to *use* it."

And he wasn't the only one. Jamie had asked Kaia's dad something similar. She wanted to *do* something—she wanted to help. And Wallace didn't say, "Study now, help out later." He told them they all had a lot to contribute.

But how would they do it? . . . Kaia wasn't sure.

"We know a lot thanks to our classes," she thought, "and knowledge is definitely a good thing to have. But the best books don't just have the best words and grammar . . . and the people who know the most aren't always the happiest. . . ."

Her eyes closed in thought—then they burst from her head.

"It isn't the knowledge . . . it's how people *use* it!"

Before Kaia knew it, she was back at her house.

After Wallace recounted his "classroom heroics" at the dinner table later that night, Cameron asked Kaia about the rest of her day.

"I think language arts was the best class today," Kaia said, tilting her head to the side. "We learned about comparative and superlative adjectives, and we worked on the worksheet in pairs."

"Superlative adjectives are the greatest of them all!" Wallace said, receiving a lighthearted elbow from Jasmine (and giggles from Kaia) for his efforts.

"Oh, and I learned about Lucas!" she continued. "He showed me his notebook—he's a writer and illustrator! And you gave him an idea for a new story, Dad!"

"Me?" Wallace asked, fingers pointed at his chest. Kaia smiled, then suddenly lowered her head.

"It's sad that he struggles in school," she said softly, "and a lot of other people do, too. Jamie's a genius and always gets A's, but she doesn't like being at school. And I'm pretty sure Dylan knows most of the answers, but he still almost never does his homework. He's not very nice to a lot of our classmates. . . ." She paused, then said slowly, "I think that he's lonely."

It was her listeners' turn to all lower their heads.

"Why can't school help us more with the other stuff?" she asked. "Stuff that makes us feel worried, or sad . . . or lonely. It's like you said, Dad, about 'well-being,' right?"

Wallace nodded her on, and Kaia continued, "Where well-being isn't important to others. . . ."

Her voice trailed off. Then she jumped from her chair. Three or four lights had turned on in her head.

"*That's it!*" she cried out. "Crisis is king!"

By then she was pacing the length of the table. She stopped— "And we have to defeat it."

Cameron stared at Kaia, wide-eyed and in wonder. Wallace felt an overwhelming urge to applaud. And with pride in her daughter's mysterious ways, Jasmine asked, "You know that what's happening isn't right . . . so what are you going to do?"

Kaia considered her options for a moment. Then, yelling, "I'll be back later . . . bye!" she sprinted down the hallway and out the front door.

If, instead of the light bulbs that lit Kaia's head, a flash bulb had captured her thoughts in a picture, it would have looked something like this.

- In a lot of ways, school overlooks our well-being.

- If schools don't do more to help lift people up, they'll serve as a playground (and breeding ground) for crisis.

- So, what should schools do—what do kids need? *What do we need to beat Crisis?*

It would take some more thinking . . . and more heads than one. Panting, she knocked on a door down the street.

"*Hola*, Kaia!" a woman said at the door.

A few seconds later she was joined by her son.

"Hi," Kaia said. "*I need your help.*"

Smiling, Lucas showed Kaia inside.

PHASE 2: PINPOINT YOUR PURPOSE
Why are we here?

You'll find that it's easier to make change together if everyone's clear on the reason you're *here*, both individually and also as a team. If you don't see the purpose, you won't make the change.

STEP 1. Why are YOU here?

Be honest and open about why you are where you are. Why are you a teacher, a principal, etc.? What is your purpose as a professional? A person?

STEP 2. Why is SCHOOL here?

Simply, what is the purpose of school? Why do kids go to school? Why does *your* school exist? Think about learners like Kaia, Lucas, Jamie, Dylan, and others in your school, in all their diversity. Is school meant to give them *all* what they need?

Compare why you're here, and the purpose of school, with what your school is in reality.

STEP 3. Why are you here with your CHANGE TEAM?

Pinpoint the purpose of your work as a Change Team. What do you hope to accomplish together?

ACTION.

Act in accordance with your purpose. Where are you successful, and what gets in the way?

CRISIS CONTROL

The following Monday morning, Kaia knocked once again at Lucas's house.

"You ready?" she asked when he opened the door.

"Ready as I'll ever be," Lucas replied, holding a thick stack of papers in his arms. He attempted to smile, but his mouth came up short.

"They're going to love it," Kaia assured him.

She truly believed it—but she felt nervous, too. It wouldn't be easy, but she knew it was worth it. "It's the right thing to do," she thought to herself. She grabbed half the papers, and they set off for Clover.

On Mondays, one of the students presented on something exciting from the past week at school. That week, the student presenting was Kaia.

Ms. Monica invited her up to begin. Kaia nodded to Lucas—and they passed out the story.

"The Depthvale Detectives?"—"This story looks awesome!"—"You did all these drawings, Lucas?!" their classmates exclaimed. Lucas's face was bright red and beaming.

Kaia and Lucas called three volunteers. Together, they read from "The Depthvale Detectives."

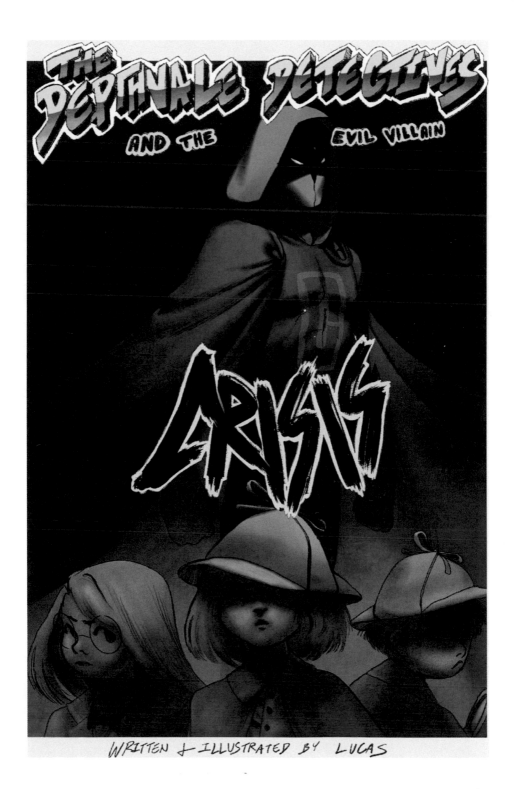

Once upon a time,
Crisis reigned over Depthvale . . .

THE VILLAIN WAS CONSTANTLY UP TO NO GOOD. WHEREVER THERE WERE PEOPLE
MAKING OTHERS' LIVES HARD, CRISIS WAS HELPING THEM DO IT.
"AND SOON" THE VILLAIN SAID "I'LL BE TOO BIG TO STOP!"

BUT ONE CLASS OF STUDENTS IN A DepthVale SCHOOL HAD THEIR OWN THINGS TO SAY ON THE MATTER. THEY SAW WHAT CRISIS WAS DOING TO THE WORLD, AND THEY SAID: "WE HAVE TO STOP HIM." SO, THEY BECAME...

THEIR MISSION WAS THIS: TO DO WHAT IT TAKES TO CONTRIBUTE TO THE WORLD AND DEFEAT CRISIS ONCE AND FOR ALL.

The story went on to tell more about crises—and to show how the villain was pulling the strings. As it turned out, not even Clover was safe.

"Even in the Depthvale Detectives' own school, Crisis was lurking in the classrooms and hallways, and outside the school on the playground," Lucas read, "trying to keep Clover's students and staff from doing the right things for others."

"But," Jamie read, "the Detectives were determined. They teamed up together for everyone at Clover, in the Depthvale community, and around the whole world, to answer the most important question of all: *What do we need to beat Crisis?*"

When those last words were spoken, the classroom erupted. The Depthvale Detectives were an instant sensation.

And the story's creator was, too. "Kaia and I wrote it together!" he insisted. But Kaia directed all praise back to Lucas.

Suddenly, a voice sounded over the noise. "Could I ask that you make your way back to your seats. . . ."

In the students' excitement, they'd forgotten one thing: *What would Ms. Monica think?*

"I just have one question," Ms. Monica said, "for Kaia and Lucas and the rest of the class—"

Her students all held their collective breath.

"What do we need to beat Crisis?" she asked. And the classroom erupted again.

THE CONTRIBUTION SOLUTION

That morning, the class started working out an answer. They saw the situation like this.

- Crisis is the ultimate negative—it takes away from people's lives.

- Crisis is defeated by **contribution**—the ultimate positive, since it adds to people's lives and to the world. Crisis brings down, and contribution lifts up.

- People feel well-being, meaning, and fulfillment in their own lives when they contribute to the well-being of others. Or, as one student aptly described it, "Making other people happy makes you happy, too!"

They were off to a good start. But they still had a problem.

"What *exactly* do we need to beat Crisis?" they wondered.

"Well," said Jamie, who, amid the excitement, was still more excited than anyone else, "we know contribution is Crisis's kryptonite." (Jamie, like Lucas, was comically inclined.) "So, if we want to know how to defeat him, we *should* ask ourselves what it takes to contribute."

Her classmates could tell she was onto something there. And Kaia was already charging ahead.

"Exactly!" she said, beaming at Jamie. "That's perfect . . . and I might have a part of the answer."

As always, Kaia had her classmates' attention. And lately, she'd been thinking a lot about Cameron.

"Lots of people don't know what's important to them, or where they fit in the world, or how to make the world better. Sometimes, we're not really sure who we *are* . . . and, when we're not, it's hard to beat Crisis. So," she concluded, "if we want to contribute, we're going to need—"

"*Self-understanding!*"

The interjection was Mason's—a close friend of Kaia's, and one of the class's more "excitable" students.

"Exactly," Kaia said, smiling still brighter. She swelled with a warm sense of pride in her class, and with more appreciation than ever before of how lucky they were to be taught by Ms. Monica.

"Bravo, class!" Ms. Monica said. "We've taken the first step in taking on Crisis. Here's what I propose we do next."

The class looked expectantly up at their teacher. "Tonight, let's be detectives—what's self-understanding? If we talk with our families and bring back our thoughts, I bet we'll get a pretty strong case put together. How does that sound to you all?" she asked.

They found it to be a fantastic idea.

Ms. Monica smiled. Then she noticed the clock—the first official meeting of the Depthvale Detectives had run through a sizeable chunk of the morning. But Ms. Monica noticed another thing, too. Her students were happy—and that was important. If their regular lessons got pushed back a little, it wasn't the end of the world.

"And maybe," she thought, "it's the start of a better one."

✳ ✳ ✳

At school the next day, the Detectives shared their findings. And soon, the whiteboard was chock-full of "evidence." Maybe, they thought, it was even *too* full—self-understanding was big and complex.

Undaunted, they started inspecting its parts. "These words go together! . . . These ideas are connected!" and similar, animated shouts filled the room as the students, crowded together by the whiteboard, took a lively approach to connecting the dots.

Before long, from the depths of the "organized chaos," the makings of self-understanding emerged.

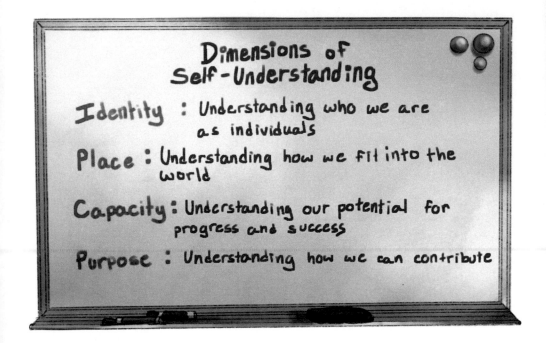

The students stood back and admired their handiwork. "Now we'll learn more about *us!*" Kaia thought.

And shortly thereafter, the students pressed on. "What *else* does it take to contribute?" they asked.

"I'm glad that you ask," Ms. Monica said, "because I'd like to propose a potential addition." Back at their desks, the class listened attentively.

"You may think I'm biased, as your teacher and all . . . but I truly believe, from the bottom of my heart, that we'll need what we're learning in each of our classes to tackle all Crisis's mischief."

At that, a chorus of groans filled the air. But Ms. Monica smiled and spoke up again.

"That's because . . ." she continued, "for so many crises, while self-understanding is just as important for deciding which problems we want to solve most, our classes will lay the foundation for solving them."

"*Check*." Kaia marked another box in her head as Ms. Monica echoed her thoughts to a T.

And while a skeptical mind might have heard in her message, "If you want to contribute, *you better do your homework*"—someone more attuned to Ms. Monica's heart would have seen the best interests of her learners at the center. To carry out their mission of taking on Crisis, there was a lot they'd need to know about the world and its workings.

"In a word," she concluded, inviting her students, "if we want to contribute, we'll also need. . . ."

"Knowledge," Jamie said. Ms. Monica nodded.

Jamie's was one of the faces that fell at Ms. Monica's mention of classwork. But when Ms. Monica explained the contributive power of pairing their knowledge and self-understanding, Jamie's eyes brightened again.

After more discussion, the students agreed (some, of course, still a little begrudgingly) that working hard in class was an absolute must—in fact, their "duty" as Depthvale Detectives.

Ms. Monica breathed a small sigh of relief. But she wasn't taking anything for granted just yet. At this stage, they couldn't risk losing momentum.

Luckily, Ms. Monica had a plan to sustain it.

– –– –– ––– ––––

The Mission Log of The Depthvale Detectives

Mission: Subject Injection
Suspects: Science, Social Studies, Language Arts
Objective: Inject each suspect with Identity, Place, Capacity, and Purpose to develop our knowledge AND self-understanding.

Field Notes:
Science. Unit: Weather and Climate. Understanding the difference between weather and climate. Comparing climates of varying geographic regions. Exploring how local weather patterns shape the Depthvale community (Focus Dimension: **Place**). Exploring the impact of weather on our lives—what do different types of weather mean to us as individuals (Focus Dimension: **Identity**)?

Social Studies. Unit: The States. Investigating what sets our state apart—what do we like and not like about it (Focus Dimensions: **Identity, Place**)? What about our state would we change for the better (Focus Dimension: **Purpose**)?

Language Arts. Unit: Verb Tenses. Using verbs to write about the past, present, and future. Writing about our pasts, important aspects of our lives in the present, and things that we'd like to do in the future (Focus Dimensions: **Identity, Place, Capacity, Purpose**).

— —— —— ——— ————

Other classes that day took on similar themes, and the students shared a lot about themselves with Ms. Monica—all in the context of curricular learning.

"Mission accomplished," she thought to herself.

But, of course, other missions lay ahead. Some students' self-understanding was limited—and, in one case, especially worrying.

"I don't know what I'm going to do in the future and I'm no good at anything anyways . . ." Dylan wrote.

Ms. Monica read through his story with sadness. "We're here to solve *their* crises, too," she reflected. And from what she could tell, there was no time to waste.

USE IT OR LOSE IT

Lessons continued in a similar vein for the next couple days in Ms. Monica's classroom—or, as it was now more commonly referred to, the Depthvale Detectives' HQ. But ever since declaring Public Enemy No. 1, the students hadn't stayed in one place very long.

"Not with Crisis at large . . ." they thought to themselves. So, they kept pressing onward.

"The stuff we've been learning is all well and good . . . but how are we really contributing?" asked Jamie. "Learning in school is just the first step. There has to be more we can *do*."

"Yeah!" Lucas said, turning to Jamie. Ever since the dawn of the Depthvale Detectives, he'd been much less shy about speaking in class. "If we keep it to ourselves, we'll never beat Crisis. We have to be able to *use* what we learn. And," he added, his face slightly red, "I bet that will help with not losing our learning."

"And not losing our minds . . ." Jamie joked quietly. She glowed with wholehearted, happy agreement.

"So," Ms. Monica guided them on, "what does it take, then, to learn—and to use it?"

Kaia thought back through their recent successes. They'd come a long way in a short span of time. What had they needed to get there?

"We wouldn't have gotten this far," Kaia said, "if Lucas hadn't thought up the Depthvale Detectives. And to come up with something so fun and imaginative . . . I think, most of all, that takes *creativity*!"

"Yeah!" Her classmates expressed their agreement—and Lucas turned bright red again.

"But I couldn't have done it alone!" he insisted. "Me and Kaia came up with the story together."

At that, Mason nearly jumped out of his seat. "Oh! Ms. Monica! I know it! I know it!" he shouted, waving his hand in the air.

Ms. Monica struggled to hold back her laughter, then warmly asked Mason to share.

"That's *collaboration*!" he practically screamed, doing little to conceal his self-satisfaction. Putting names to ideas was proving delightful.

"I've got another one!" Tori exclaimed, after all had agreed with Mason's addition. "It's simple, really . . . we're doing it right now. . . ."

The riddle was lost on the rest of the class.

"Talking!" she said with an air of annoyance, as if nothing in the world could be any more obvious. "It's fun, for one, and it's also really helpful. If you have something important to say, talk about it!"

Tori, suffice it to say, talked a lot—about the important and unimportant alike.

Ms. Monica smiled and uncapped her marker, adding *communication* to their list on the whiteboard.

With the help of some more communication (or, talking) and a lively collaborative effort from the class, their ideas of having to "think hard" and "work hard" were grounded into two final whiteboard additions, altogether comprising five critical competencies.

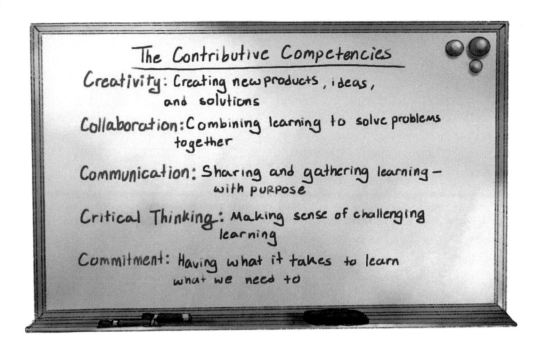

The Contributive Competencies

Creativity: Creating new products, ideas, and solutions

Collaboration: Combining learning to solve problems together

Communication: Sharing and gathering learning — with purpose

Critical Thinking: Making sense of challenging learning

Commitment: Having what it takes to learn what we need to

"*Self-understanding, knowledge,* and *competency,*" thought the class, taking some time to look over their progress.

It was true . . . they had come a long way.

LEARN AND RETURN

While the close of the week found the students sky high, the weekend was a little more troubling for Kaia.

At home, Wallace still seemed out of sorts. He watched Channel 9 every day without fail, and Kaia could tell what he saw wore him down.

"Funny enough," he told Kaia one evening, "it's almost enough to make me wish I was there."

Cameron had been in a funk of his own—especially, Kaia noticed, in the past couple weeks. When she asked him one night if there was anything wrong, he told her, "I wish I had something to *add.* . . ."

"But you do!" she insisted. She knew it firsthand—what he'd already added for Kaia alone was more than most sisters could expect in a lifetime.

She resolved to help Cameron however she could. "He helps me every day and in so many ways. . . . What can I do in return?"

✳ ✳ ✳

Back at HQ the following Monday, the Detectives adapted to School 2.0. Whereas before it was only about content and knowledge, now it was all about contributing back. One Kaia-coined phrase seemed to capture it best. No matter the curricular focus at hand, they stuck to the motto, *"Learn and return!"* All of the students could get behind that.

Now, when Ms. Monica taught or observed, she no longer talked about knowledge alone, but self-understanding and competency, too, in just the same way as curricular content. They were learning a new language—and the class caught on quick.

Wanting to share (and, for good reason, show off) their competency, knowledge, and self-understanding, the Detectives put a thrilling new mission in motion.

Ms. Monica's Classroom Presents:
The Depthvale Detectives vs.
the Evil Villain Crisis

What: A marvelous multi-act performance
When: Last Friday of the month
Where: Clover Auditorium
Why: To bring the mission of the Depthvale Detectives to life for our parents, families, and friends.

For the people of Depthvale and all over the world, one name strikes more fear in our hearts than any other: CRISIS.

Crisis works hard to keep good people down, and to keep us from doing the right things for others. And if our schools and communities can't take Crisis on, there's no telling what he might do to the world. . . .

But no need to fear—the DETECTIVES are here! Our new learning journey is equipping every one of us with everything we need to solve all kinds of crises, from personal troubles, to the struggles of others, to BIG problems threatening every one of us globally. In this magical, marvelous, multi-act performance, we'll show you how all of our learning comes together to tackle the crises that stand in our way.

Come one, come all to a night out to dive in—to the Depthvale Detectives, our plot against Crisis, and the power of using our learning for good.

In the weeks spent preparing for the students' performance, Ms. Monica came to her class with a challenge. Following a math lesson one afternoon, she gave them a handout that covered the lesson, and then asked for responses to one simple prompt: *"How can you show that you understand integers?"*

When they shared their responses, Ms. Monica beamed—her students' creativity was a sight to behold. And whenever they took that approach from then on, they referred to it simply as "Show That You Know."

"How's *that* for self-assessment," Ms. Monica thought, brimming with well-deserved pride in their progress.

Just then, looking back up from her desk, her eyes fell on Kaia, Lucas, and Jamie, huddled together in a corner of the classroom.

"What are they up to? . . ." she thought to herself.

It didn't stay shrouded in mystery long. Seconds later, the three made their way to her desk.

"Ms. Monica," Jamie said, taking the lead, "we've been doing some thinking." They had her attention. "Putting on a performance is a great way to start, and we know that the people who watch it will love it. But we have to keep getting our messages out! And we think there's a way we can do it."

Ms. Monica smiled and nodded her on.

"Kaia's dad sparked my thinking," Jamie continued, "and now that we're taking on Crisis together, the three of us think it's the right thing to do." She shuffled in place for a moment, then asked, "Can we start a news network at Clover?"

Ms. Monica slowly leaned back in her chair. "I think that that sounds like a wonderful idea."

The three pumped their fists and together cried, "*Yes!*"

"And we already have some ideas!" Lucas shouted, stumbling over his words from excitement. "Jamie's lead anchor, and Kaia's producer. . . ."

"And you?" Ms. Monica asked with a smile.

Lucas assumed a determined expression. "It's time to bring the Depthvale Detectives to the screen," he said boldly. Kaia and Jamie both nodded.

"It certainly is," Ms. Monica smiled. She looked to the network's producer expectantly. "So . . . what's the first order of business?"

Kaia considered for an instant, then answered, "Putting the rest of the News Team together!"

"Now, *that* is production!" Ms. Monica said, as the three students happily giggled along. "If the rest of the team are like you three," she added, "your show will go right to the top!"

Later that day, Ms. Monica gave Kaia, Lucas, and Jamie a chance to pitch CloverTV to their classmates. In no time, the class bubbled over with excitement. They volunteered Mason as lead sports reporter (to which he immediately, and proudly, consented). And when someone suggested they should use social media, every head in the room swiveled 'round to one person.

"No need to ask," Tori waved up her palm, accepting the role as her preordained duty. "I'm already on it," she added, and smiled.

Almost everyone offered to help in some way, with one very glaring exception—Dylan.

Kaia remembered a scene from that morning. In the parking lot, Dylan climbed out from his car, pulled out his backpack, and slammed the door shut. But before the door closed Kaia made out the words, ". . . Dylan, why can't you do anything right?! If you keep on like this . . . you'll be good for nothing! . . ."

As the network was first introduced to the class, Kaia thought Dylan had looked almost hopeful. But as each role was mentioned, and as, one by one, the students all volunteered others to fill them, Dylan's expression grew darker and darker.

"Anyone else?" Kaia looked at him hopefully. But Dylan stared down at his desk in dark silence.

BREAKING NEWS

"Kaia!"

She whipped back her head in the direction of the call, and saw Jamie and Tori hiding out by the bushes. A few days had passed since the network announcement, and class was about to begin for the day.

Kaia ran to her friends. "What is it?" she asked. She could tell that whatever it was, it wasn't good.

"He put it online . . ." Tori said, looking down. "I showed it to my mom, and she said she'd call his parents. . . . I feel so bad for him, Kaia. It's awful."

Slowly, she pulled out her phone from her pocket. She turned it toward Kaia—and Dylan appeared. Kaia's heart sank to the pit of her stomach.

"This just in!" Dylan yelled in the video.

He was dressed in a button-down shirt and a tie, and sitting with both of his arms on a desk. He paused for a moment and adjusted some papers, then boomed, *"THE WORLD IS A TERRIBLE PLACE."*

"Oh, no . . ." Kaia whispered. She leaned against Jamie.

"What's even the point?!" Dylan screamed through his teeth. *"Nothing good ever happens . . . so why even try?"*

He paused as his eyes dropped away from the camera. *"There's nowhere in the world I belong . . ."* he said slowly, *"not at home, or my neighborhood, or anywhere at all. . . ."*

Color came rushing to his face on the screen. "*And school . . .*" he continued, clenching his jaw, "*school is the worst place of all.*"

He had mean words for Clover—and for most of his classmates. They grated against Kaia's ears as she listened.

"*Everyone thinks that I'm dumb . . .*" Dylan said. "*Well, guess what? . . . Lucas is dumber!*" He attempted to smile, but his lips shook too violently. "*And the Depthvale Detectives are dumbest of all. . . .*"

After speaking those words, tears streamed from his eyes.

"*Crisis is going to win,*" he said slowly, earlier anger replaced now with sadness. "*Because . . . he always does.*"

At that, Dylan rose with a visible effort, walked to the camera—and the screen cut to black.

When Dylan walked into the classroom that morning, Kaia felt a deafening hush fill the room.

Ms. Monica sensed the disturbance as well. She opened by asking, "Everything good?" Not getting much in reply from her students, she frowned, and then scanned the seats.

"No Lucas, today . . ." she said to herself, jotting the note with the rest of attendance. And with housekeeping settled, they kicked off the day.

But that day felt different than the others before it. And Kaia, at frequent and regular intervals, stole sad looks at Lucas's bare, empty desk.

* * *

On her way home from school, Kaia stopped by at Lucas's.

"Hi . . ." Kaia said when he opened the door, "we missed you at school today."

Lucas said nothing. He stood by the door and looked down at his shoes.

"I'm sorry, Lucas . . ." she said. But he smiled.

"It's okay," Lucas said, "I'm feeling much better." A huge weight was lifted from Kaia's small shoulders.

"It hurt," he went on, "but people have helped me. First my mom, and now you." Kaia blushed in the doorway. "But *he* doesn't have anybody right now . . . and I think that's what hurts most of all."

Neither friend spoke for a moment or two.

"I actually *like* it at school now," he continued, "thanks to our friends and the new things we're doing." He paused and considered his words for a moment. "If there's one thing I've learned . . . I want Dylan to be happy."

Kaia looked at her friend with a new sense of wonder. Then, bringing her hands to her hips, she said:

"This sounds like a job for the Depthvale Detectives."

--- --- --- --- ----

The Mission Log of the Depthvale Detectives

Mission: Lift-Up
Target Code Name: Anchor/Detective
Tools: Self-Understanding ✔   Knowledge ✔   Competency ✔
Objective: Belonging.
Priority: 1

Time Log:
Thursday, 3:27 p.m.: Kaia and Lucas enter Lucas's house.

Thursday, 4:17 p.m.: Jamie's dad drops off Jamie at Lucas's house.

Thursday, 6:46 p.m.: Jamie's dad arrives back at Lucas's house. Kaia and Jamie both get in the car.

Friday, 8:53 a.m.: Kaia, Lucas, and Jamie meet on the playground at Clover. The three detectives converse, while Lucas writes in his notebook.

Friday, 8:58 a.m.: Lucas tears out a page from his notebook, runs across the playground to the tetherball court, and tapes the piece of paper to the ball.

Friday, 8:59:57 a.m.: Breathless, Kaia, Lucas, and Jamie take their seats. Three seconds later, the morning bell rings.

— —— —— ——— ————

Ms. Monica welcomed her class for the day. But just like they had been the morning before, her students were unusually quiet.

"Something is up . . ." she thought to herself. And if she couldn't work it out before long, she decided, she'd have to start asking some questions.

It was as if the excitement of their past weeks had vanished. And, for Ms. Monica, it was all too familiar. "No . . ." she thought, "we're not going back."

The mid-morning bell came as welcome relief, and the students filed out of the classroom to recess.

* * *

Dylan walked wearily out to the playground, head down and muttering under his breath. From his talk with his parents the evening before, and from the way all his classmates averted their eyes, he suspected they'd all seen the video by then. And anyway, he thought, what did it matter?

"They hated me then, they still hate me now . . ." he muttered as he made for his corner of the playground. The sky was dark, and the wind was swirling. It looked like a storm was approaching.

Dylan trudged to the tetherball court, grabbed the ball—and noticed a note hanging off it.

Naturally, Dylan's curiosity prevailed. He turned a sharp corner past the fence by the slide and saw Kaia, Lucas, and Jamie by the swing.

The second he saw them, Dylan turned on his heels.

"Wait!" Kaia pleaded. "Dylan . . . *we need you!*"

"What do you want?!" Dylan shouted, turning back.

"We'll never beat Crisis without you!" Kaia said. "It'll take every one of us, and a whole lot more. We need you to help get the word out to everyone!"

"How am I supposed to do *that*?" he cried hopelessly, with heartbreaking pain and desperation in his voice.

But Jamie, in his moment of need, had an answer. She walked up to Dylan, then said with assurance: "I want you to be my co-anchor."

In the silence that followed, Dylan stood stunned. His eyes moved from Jamie, to Kaia, to Lucas—who hadn't yet moved from his spot by the swing.

But right then he made his way over to Dylan and gave him the page he'd been holding in his hand. It was a drawing of Dylan, as Anchor and Detective.

Dylan stared at the drawing then back up at Lucas, as soft tears of joy filled the wells of his eyes.

* * *

"Ms. Monica," Kaia said, back in class after recess, "I think we're still missing one piece of the puzzle."

Eager for anything that might change the mood, Ms. Monica smiled and urged Kaia on.

"We're already in a great place," Kaia said. "Against Crisis, we need self-understanding, knowledge, *and* competency. But if that's all we have . . ." she paused for a moment, "who's to say that we'll use all our powers for *good*?"

She could tell that the class didn't totally follow. So, she continued explaining out loud.

"Contributing is making a *positive* difference. It's making people happy, and making the world better. If we have self-understanding, knowledge, and competency, but then don't feel close to other people or the world . . . well . . ." she continued, "we'd be forces for evil."

Mason was visibly shaken by the turn. "Yeah . . . we'd be Crisis's henchmen!" he shouted. The rest of the class expressed similar concern.

"So," Ms. Monica said, speaking slowly, "what do you think is the one missing link? What do we need to be forces for good?"

Kaia gave Dylan an encouraging smile.

He raised up his hand. "*Connection*," he said.

And, for the moment, his classmates' misgivings were replaced with unanimous, happy agreement.

Kaia's eyes glistened as they watched her new friend. The smile that lit Dylan's face wasn't cold, or callous, or sneering, or at others' expense—it was warm, sincere, and endlessly grateful.

Already experienced at the art of dissection, the Detectives put the last puzzle pieces in place.

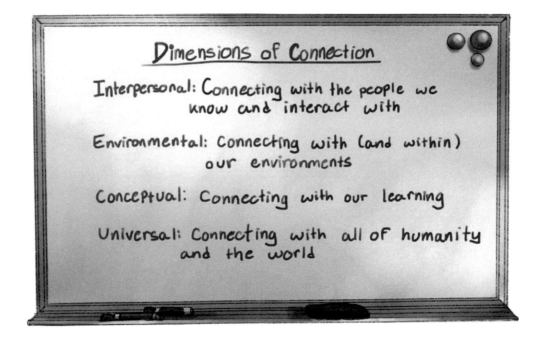

At afternoon recess, Dylan made the rounds.

Some classmates were wary and skeptical at first, but deep down they felt things were going to be different. It would take some more time—Dylan had dug a deep hole—but his words were remorseful, heartfelt, and kind.

Not long before heading back in after recess, he walked to the tree in the corner of the playground, where Lucas sat working on a new illustration.

With tears in his eyes, Dylan told him, *"I'm sorry. . . ."*

But Lucas was motioning Dylan to join him. "Can you help me come up with ideas?" he asked. "I'm writing more stories about the Depthvale Detectives. . . ."

Dylan may never have felt quite so good. Too happy for words, he sat down with Lucas.

And Kaia, with a glance at her friends, jumped for joy.

The pieces were in place, the class was connected—and Crisis was shaking in his villainous boots.

PHASE 3: DIVE INTO OUTCOMES
What do we want?

People want well-being, meaning, and fulfillment, both for themselves and for others around them. But what gives us well-being, meaning, and fulfillment? Or, what do we need in our lives to beat Crisis?

As Kaia and each of her classmates explored, **contribution** links learning with lifelong success. And if we all want to add, we *all* need the outcomes.

(***Note:** *In this phase and each of the others, keep in mind that these steps will take time. You don't have to work through them all in one sitting. Instead, take the time to dive deeply together.*)

STEP 1. *Reflect.*
With your team, reflect on the journey of the Depthvale Detectives from **self-understanding**, to **knowledge** and **competency**, and, finally, through to **connection**. Talk about each individual outcome—what they mean for you, and what they might mean for your school.

STEP 2. *Dissect.*
Access the **Learning Progressions** at www.depthvaledetectives.com. These tools are measures of learning. One measure at a time, dive deeply into each outcome individually, and then discuss your findings with your team. What do you see, and what do they tell you?

STEP 3. *Measure.*

Contributive learning is about *your* well-being too—because it's hard to give students what you don't have yourself. So, for one, some, or each learning outcome, use the Learning Progressions to measure where you are. What evidence are you using to determine your ratings? (Also, take time to think about knowledge. In what ways are you knowledgeable, and what would you like to be more knowledgeable about?) Then, share with your team.

Remember to keep the Four Pillars in mind, and think about how to make progress together—not only as a Change Team, but also with your students. You're *all* working closely toward the same learning outcomes.

STEP 4. *Design.*

Discuss "Subject Injection," "Show That You Know," and "The Depthvale Detectives vs. the Evil Villain Crisis." How do they lend themselves to contributive learning? Think about (and, if possible, design) simple ways of "injecting" your own school's experiences with self-understanding, knowledge, competency, and connection.

ACTION.

Choose one dimension of one outcome as a focus. For one student (or, alternatively, for yourself) pay attention to evidence of that dimension in their learning. Where are they now, and how can they progress?

THE STAGE IS SET

Around that time at Clover, different members of the community had different ideas about what was happening in Ms. Monica's classroom. Those ideas looked something like this.

Students. It had already been an incredible ride. They'd never felt closer to one another (or their teacher), and they actually *liked* what they worked on at school—a realization from which, unsurprisingly enough, many of the students hadn't fully recovered. While they didn't know exactly what all of it would lead to, all they imagined were endless contributions. They wanted to learn, and they wanted to *add*.

Parents. Gathering information about their kids' days had once felt like pulling out teeth. Now, stories spilled from their mouths. But those stories didn't sound much like "school" to the parents, and some were understandably skeptical. *"There must be a catch . . ."* they thought to themselves. *"Are they learning what they need to? Will they be ready for next year?"* They monitored grades more closely than ever. After all, they wanted their kids to succeed.

School Staff. Ms. Monica's class was a bit of an enigma. The rest of the staff could tell *something* was up, but not knowing what put a few ill at ease. These were the teachers with noses for change (or, as it registered to their senses, disturbance). It was their job to sniff out—and snuff out—the scent.

Ms. Monica. Rather than leaving her drained and discombobulated, the weeks that had passed gave her energy and direction. She knew what her class had been doing was meaningful. And teaching, for her, had never been more fulfilling. But, like her students, she still wanted more. "Something this good can't be kept to ourselves. . . ."

Luckily, it wouldn't stay secret for long. The night they'd been waiting for had finally arrived.

The crowd made their way into Clover's auditorium, excited to see what the night had in store. Kaia's grandfather may have been happiest of all. He laughed with his grandson, daughter, and son-in-law as they all took their seats at the start of the night.

And it wasn't just families and friends in attendance. Some teachers came, too, and even Principal Moseley, true to the promise he'd made to the students.

Ms. Monica peeked from behind the drawn curtain at the roomful of people sitting ready in their seats. She took a deep breath, and stepped out on the stage.

"Welcome!" Ms. Monica boomed through the microphone, in a voice much befitting a master of ceremonies, "to a night brought to you by the Depthvale Detectives. There's so much I could say about each of these students . . . but tonight, I'll let them do the talking.

"And so, without further ado," she continued, "allow me to present the event you've been waiting for—*The Depthvale Detectives vs. the Evil Villain Crisis!*"

With a flourish Ms. Monica strode from the stage as the curtain opened up to reveal . . . Crisis, crouching alone on the stage in the spotlight.

Under the detailed, hand-crafted costume, Lucas's heart beat a mile a minute. But, in the moment of truth, he was ready.

"Behold!" Lucas bellowed, brandishing his cape, "the most evil and fearsome of all the world's villains . . . the one who will see to humanity's demise!"

Lucas crept nimbly across the dark stage. "Wherever there are people who are up to no good, I am there smiling and guiding their hands. . . . Wherever there are people who are down on their luck, I am there laughing and keeping them low. . . . Wherever there is anything wrong in the world . . . I am the cause, and I am the outcome!"

His monologue had its desired effect—every eye in the audience was glued to the speaker.

"My name," he said coldly, "though all here have met me. . . ." He paused, and the crowd felt a chill fill the air. "My name," he thundered, "is CRISIS!"

At that, the lights on the stage cut to black, drawing some genuine gasps from the crowd.

Some long seconds passed. Then, through the darkness: "Soon the whole world will do Crisis's bidding . . . and nothing and no one can stop—"

"*Not so fast!*"

A chorus of voices rang out from the stage, and the spotlight beamed down on a team of detectives, made up of Kaia, Jamie, and Dylan.

Dylan took a confident step toward the audience. "We are the Depthvale Detectives!" he shouted. "First line of defense against Crisis and his henchmen. And until he no longer wreaks havoc and mayhem, it's our sworn assignment to meet him head on!"

"And our mission," added Jamie, "is well underway...."

The audience roared as the curtain came down. Suffice it to say, they were already hooked.

And over the course of the rest of the evening, as the students in their acts tackled all kinds of crises, the Detectives, up against Crisis's villainy, had what they needed to foil his plans.

The final act featured the cast of the first. And the opening sequence looked a little like this.

IN SCHOOLS, ONLINE, AND OUT IN THE COMMUNITY, BULLYING IS HARMING BOTH KIDS AND ADULTS — AND CRISIS IS CAUSING IT ALL. JAMIE AND DYLAN, HE HAS TO BE STOPPED.

The stage lights cut out. And when they flashed back on, the anchors had changed into Depthvale Detectives. They ran from the stage in the direction of Crisis, and used what they'd learned to stop bullying in its tracks.

When the students emerged at the end of the show, Lucas' mom had tears in her eyes. Dylan was smothered in hugs by his parents, and when Kaia got back to her grandpa, he told her, "Crisis has nothing on students like you!" He asked if at some point she'd come to his nursing home to read them the story of the Depthvale Detectives, and Kaia brimmed over with unbridled joy.

When the night finally came to an unwanted end, only Principal Moseley and Ms. Monica remained.

"Well, Ms. Monica," said Principal Moseley, "I've been waiting for something like this for a while. At our staff meeting Tuesday, can you share what you're doing?" Ms. Monica said she'd be happy to share.

"In all of my years," Principal Moseley continued, "I've never learned more from a single event."

He turned, and she twirled once around on her toes. They locked up the doors and parted ways for the weekend.

THE COUNCIL OF CLOVER

"It's now or never . . ." thought Principal Moseley.

And he really believed it—the school was in trouble. But the first-year principal hadn't given up hope. So, at the staff meeting following the performance, he took a deep breath, and put it all on the line.

"Today," he began, shortly into the meeting, "Ms. Monica's going to tell us a story. I hope it'll spark some discussion among us, along with new hopes for our school for the future. Because I see this as a truly defining moment for Clover. Whatever we do . . . it's from now on."

He paused, and then nodded his head to Ms. Monica. "Over to you," he said with a smile. Ms. Monica thanked him, then kicked off the story.

She started way back at the very beginning, when crisis was something her students saw everywhere but often felt hopeless to do anything about. Then she talked about Crisis and the Depthvale Detectives, learning to contribute, and, proudly, her students.

"We all have a Lucas," Ms. Monica said, "who lights up our days and has so much ability but struggles with the outcomes we're required to report on. And students like Jamie, at the top of the class, but who'd rather be anywhere other than the classroom. And Dylan, who just need a little connection . . . and Kaia, who bring out what's best in us all.

"We're doing them *all* a disservice," she continued, "until they all get what they need."

Some of the staff members nodded their agreement. And Principal Moseley picked up on the thread. "Students need more than most schools have been giving them. We *can* put their well-being first, but we don't. And *that*," his voice rose and then lowered again, "might actually be the worst crisis of all."

Slowly, his words sunk their way through the room. They were met with feelings of eagerness and excitement—along with reluctance, nervousness, and fear.

"How would things change in the life of the school? . . . What would this mean for our teaching?" thought the staff. Still, to that point (and Ms. Monica's delight), they all appeared open to at least hearing more.

Then a voice sounded. "*Ahem . . . if I may. . . .*"

It belonged to a teacher with sharp, pointed features, who sat with arms folded at the head of the table.

"Please, Ms. Melder," said Principal Moseley, inviting the teacher to share.

Coldly, she began, "I may be mistaken . . . but isn't this *school*?"

Some heads slowly wilted.

"Our job, last I checked, is to teach the curriculum. If we don't," she shot a sharp glance around the room, "I don't have to tell you what's going to happen."

"You're right, Ms. Melder," Ms. Monica replied. "We *should* teach the curriculum, because knowledge is important. But it's not all we need to feel meaning and fulfillment and to change people's lives and the world for the better. And *that* is what school is . . . well, should be . . . about."

Color came rising to Ms. Melder's face. "You're saying that what we've been doing with students, for all of these years, is suddenly *wrong*? This is the way things have always been done," she said slowly, emphasizing each word. "And just look at the leaders this school has produced! You can't truly mean that we're giving them nothing."

Principal Moseley leaned back in his chair. Despite his continuing efforts that year, his staff had been wary to raise new ideas. The root of that problem was increasingly clear—and, at that moment, red in the face.

"Nothing? No . . ." Principal Moseley responded. "There's a lot that we give them . . . and there's more we can do.

"It's true," he went on, "the sun keeps on shining, the world keeps on turning . . . kids still go to school. The urgency isn't that easy to see. Still, we're surrounded by crisis, inequity, broken communities, unhappy students. . . . If we're looking for urgency, we should open our eyes."

His words struck a chord, and the staff nodded slowly.

"We won't solve the problem today," he continued, "but it's hard to imagine letting one day go by where we're not working toward the solution. So, I propose that we form up a *team*, whose single driving purpose is our students' well-being.

"Would anyone else like to join me?" he asked.

Ms. Monica nodded. Three others did, too. And Ms. Melder still steamed at the head of the table.

But she wasn't done yet. "I'd like to join. . . ."

Some saw her lips form a sinister smile. But Principal Moseley saw more to the story. "Good," he thought, "we won't get there without her."

He thanked the volunteers, and the staff parted ways.

THIS IS HOW YOU CHANGE TEAM

Ms. Melder strode silently down the long hallway.

The staff meeting left her a little unsettled, but she'd seen it all in her years at the school (including five principals in the past ten alone). "Change comes as it will and soon falls by the wayside . . . and this time won't be any different," she thought. So she figured she'd watch—and assist—the demise.

Reaching the office at the end of the hallway, she knocked twice and opened the door. Ms. Melder was the last of the six to arrive. She walked to her seat, and the meeting began.

"Welcome, *Change Team*," said Principal Moseley. All but Ms. Melder smiled warmly at the name.

Simply, he told them his vision for the Change Team: to discover what kids really need to succeed, and to help lead the changes together from there.

"But today," he said, "we're just getting started. So, let's all get to know who we are." For the rest of the meeting, that's what they did.

PHASE 1: START WITH YOURSELVES

There was more left to learn at the close of the meeting. In fact, Ms. Melder hadn't shared much at all. But, as a whole, the Change Team grew closer—finally, they all got to know one another.

The Clover School Change Team

Principal Moseley. Speaking of extracurricular interests, he said to the Change Team, "I try to keep busy. . . ." From what they could tell, he did a good job. If he wasn't volunteering his time in the community, he was likely out biking, fishing, or hiking, or otherwise "putting my hands to good use." His hands often gripped either paper or pen—he was never too busy to read or to write.

Ms. Monica. She grew up in Depthvale with three younger siblings, who all felt incredibly lucky to have her. Ms. Monica brought the same care to her teaching—"If my siblings and students are happy, then I am." Her free time was filled up with endless activity—exercise, artwork, time spent with friends. . . . To all her activity she gave herself willingly. And, in return, life gave her energy.

Mr. B. No one at Clover was more down to earth, and no one had quite as much fun with their students. "It's their last year at Clover," he said of his 8th graders, "and my job to send them off right." By all accounts, that's what he did. Mr. B. was a homebody, but none the less busy for it. There was always a project or three in the works, a meal in the oven, and music in the air. Guitar, violin, banjo, piano—each night, the instruments' sounds filled the house. "My hands always say the right things," he explained, and he laughed in his easy, good-natured way.

Mrs. McCarthy. Clover's librarian was fifty years married, mother to three lucky middle-aged children, and grandma to twelve "little urchins" to boot (though some, she admitted, were grownups themselves). In effect, she had dozens more grandkids than that—the students adored her, and she adored them. But if anyone got half a mind not to read . . . "Well, I tell them the truth—read or rot!" Mrs. McCarthy was active in the community, had already traveled all over the world, and harbored no shortage of plans for the future. "Better do it while I'm young!" she'd say with a smile. If that was her timeline, there was no need to hurry.

Jack. Clover's 3rd grade teacher and resident tech expert never spent too long away from computers. Gaming, coding, developing websites—Jack had a mind for it all. And, at Clover, he put it to work. "Tech gets the students excited," he said, "and when they're excited, they're ready to learn." Even Ms. Monica's students were attached to the shy, quiet teacher who helped with their tech. And Jack, at least in the eyes of the students, was quickly becoming attached to Ms. Monica. . . . As he shared about himself with the rest of the Change Team, whenever their eyes met his face altered color.

Ms. Melder. When her turn came to share, Ms. Melder said little about who she was. Instead, she reminded them what she'd been doing—"Teaching for longer than *you've* been alive." (She pointed out all except Mrs. McCarthy.) In fairness, she had been at Clover a while. Actually, longer than anyone else. But outside their professional experiences together, none of her colleagues knew anything about her. She didn't have any close relationships at Clover—or, for all they knew, anywhere else. . . .

✳   ✳   ✳

The following week, the team met again. This time, equipped with a better understanding of who they'd be "Change Teaming" with moving forward, they were ready to add another focus to the mix.

"Alright, team," said Principal Moseley, "tell me . . . why are we here?" It turned out to be a big question.

PHASE 2: PINPOINT YOUR PURPOSE

On the surface, the answer seemed simple enough—they wanted to make a difference in the lives of their kids. But they also wanted kids to be successful in school. . . .

"Sadly, there's a difference," remarked Mr. B. "Sometimes I get so concerned with kids' grades, with trying to help them do well in their classes . . . that I lose sight of other things happening in their lives. Things that are just as important—at least. It's the sad truth we're living with," Mr. B. sighed. "School's less about lives than it is about grades."

Mrs. McCarthy was on the same page. "I know what I *want* for my own kids and grandkids. It's sure a lot more than they get from their schools."

"It's just like Ms. Monica said," Jack jumped in. "We all want our kids to feel meaning and fulfillment and to change people's lives and the world for the better. If we know what we want, then why ask for less?"

No one could come up with any good reasons. Though a few not-so-good ones crossed Ms. Melder's mind. . . .

"My time will come," she thought to herself. So, in the meantime, she sat there in silence.

But the others set to work. And at the end of the meeting, the team put a summary of their thoughts on the whiteboard.

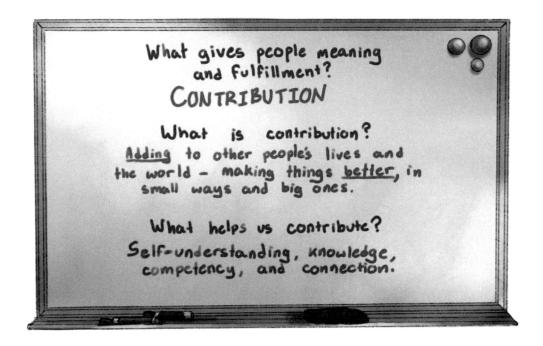

What gives people meaning and fulfillment?
CONTRIBUTION

What is contribution?
Adding to other people's lives and the world — making things better, in small ways and big ones.

What helps us contribute?
Self-understanding, knowledge, competency, and connection.

"Well, team," Principal Moseley began, "our purpose is practically popping off the board."

Ms. Monica smiled in anticipation. "As a school, as individuals, as a community—as *people*," he continued, "our purpose is this."

He picked out a bright-colored marker from the bin and circled the word "CONTRIBUTION."

Ms. Monica cheered. Jack started clapping. And Mrs. McCarthy yelled, "Hip hip, hooray!" Mr. B. sunk back down in his chair from exertion. "Now, *this* is how you Change Team!" he said with a smile.

Their purpose shone clearer than ever before.

When their next scheduled meeting came rolling around, Jack took a look at the school's Purpose Picture. "There's no contribution without self-understanding, knowledge, competency, and connection," he said.

His principal nodded. "Then we know where to start."

PHASE 3: DIVE INTO OUTCOMES

The Change Team unpacked the four outcomes in their picture. And thanks to the help of Ms. Monica's students, there was a lot there already to build from.

As they fleshed out the outcomes and described their dimensions, Mrs. McCarthy shared a sudden observation.

"Ya know," she began, "I've been alive for a while." Discreetly, the others on the team exchanged smiles. "So . . . you can trust me on this one." She smiled, then pointing to the outcomes in their picture, said slowly, "These are what matter throughout our whole lives. Self-understanding, knowledge, competency, connection—from zero to a hundred, they're what get you through the day."

"That sure is the truth," Mr. B. replied softly. "In fact, if we want to help students in these areas . . . well, we should probably start with ourselves."

The others agreed. So they gave it a try. And, at times, the conversation was challenging.

Ms. Monica shared about struggles with mindfulness, and Jack with self-doubt, indecision, and purpose. Mrs. McCarthy saw her husband's health fading, and she wished that their kids were a little more attentive. Mr. B. told the team (before anyone else) about troubles communicating with his college-age son. And Principal Moseley longed more than anything for the lifelong connection he still hadn't found.

But for most of the meeting the Change Team was smiling—they lifted each other whenever they could. They were happy to have other people to share with, and to now have the chance to progress with each other—and, they soon realized, with their students as well.

"When we get our first taste of this stuff in the classroom, I'm guessing we're in for a good one, Ms. Monica?"

Ms. Monica smiled at Jack in reply.

All the while, Ms. Melder sat sullenly brooding. Whenever she answered the others' invitations with anything more than a shake of the head, "Nothing to add" was all she would say.

ADDITION, SUBTRACTION

While the Change Team discussed ways of teaching and learning, the Depthvale Detectives were hard at work, too. They were learning with purpose—and making preparations.

— ·— ·— ·—· ·—··

The Mission Log of the Depthvale Detectives

Mission: Launch
Objective: Get CloverTV off the ground.

Recruits:

Jack. General tech support. Ongoing support for the CloverTV Web Development Team.

Mrs. McCarthy. Research consultant. Direct CloverTV staff to relevant articles/books.

Mr. B. Music coordinator. Assist CloverTV Music Team with theme/show music.

Principal Moseley. Content consultant. Work closely with staff and Ms. Monica on news content/stories.

Wallace. Journalism/reporting support. Conduct in-class experiences with links to Language Arts.

Jasmine. Host graphic design workshops. Work closely with cast and crew of *The Depthvale Detectives.*

Cameron. CloverTV Film Team manager. Teach proper use of video equipment. Assist with all filming and interviews. Run afterschool CloverTV elective.

The Channel 9 News Team. Mentor CloverTV News Team and other staff during field trip to Channel 9 headquarters.

— —— —— ——— ————

And the list of recruits went on and on. Tori's mom helped her daughter's Social Media Team launch a targeted, cross-platform marketing campaign, not that they needed much help to begin with. And other kids' parents, and others in the community, got in on the act, too.

* * *

One morning, in the middle of Ms. Monica's lesson, Jamie laid her forehead on the top of her desk. Then, rising slowly, she stretched out her hand.

"Ms. Monica . . ." she said, thinly veiling vexation, "when will we ever use *this?*"

Judging by looks from a lot of her classmates, many, like Jamie, didn't quite see the point. They looked apprehensively up at Ms. Monica.

But Ms. Monica smiled. She finally had an answer.

"I'm glad that you asked that, Jamie," she said. "When you leave school, a lot of you (maybe even all of you) won't need to solve any problems like this. . . . But every last one of us will need to solve problems."

Ms. Monica watched as understanding set in.

"Even if we don't use this *knowledge*," she continued, "the *competencies* we'll need to develop in the process are useful no matter what problem we're solving. And if we collaborate with others as we work through the learning, the *connections* we form could last us a lifetime. And whether you find this stuff interesting or boring, either way you're developing *self-understanding*.

"At the end of the day," Ms. Monica concluded, "you're learning a lot more than what's on the page."

Jamie could easily get behind that. "We'll always face challenging problems . . . that's life!"

"And there's all kinds of ways we can solve them!" added Lucas.

"And there's *nothing* we can't solve together," Kaia said.

Ms. Monica looked at her students and smiled. "*Contributive learning* makes all the difference. Thanks, class, for showing me." The class thanked her back.

"Long live the Depthvale Detectives!" Dylan yelled. And everyone cheered in return.

✳ ✳ ✳

The students all felt they were still just beginning—but others had sights firmly fixed on the *end*. To them, it was only a matter of time. . . .

At their regular meeting later that day, the Change Team examined another key question.

"We know what we want," Principal Moseley began, pointing to the outcomes in the school's Purpose Picture. "So, where are we now?"

PHASE 4: PLOT YOUR POSITION

Since joining together, the team paid attention. They watched what was happening within Clover's walls, and they witnessed a lot that was already good. But contributive learning was patchy at best, because everything outside their own inclinations told teachers it wasn't their purpose. And that, understandably, got everyone down.

Up rose a culture of instruction, not learning—of boundaries, not belonging—and so, of crisis, not contribution.

In a culture like theirs, change wouldn't come quickly. But the Change Team was ready to do what was needed. And that, for starters, meant checking objections.

Notes from Change Team Meeting #4
Objection Checking — What's Stopping Us?

"There's not enough time." This is a big one. Let's highlight the meaning of MORE vs. DIFFERENT. Doing more things vs. doing things differently. This is the latter. It's not about add-ons, it's about a new lens—a lens over all that we do. Also, START SMALL—learn something new about <u>one</u> of your students and do something positive with what you discover. You'll only want more after that.

"That's not my job." <u>Old Job Description</u>—teach the curriculum. <u>New Job Description</u>—teach the curriculum, connect with your students, discover who they are, and help them contribute. That's a little more meaningful . . . and a lot more fulfilling.

"The system doesn't value these outcomes, anyway." Maybe not yet, but <u>we</u> can—and have to. If we want our students to contribute tomorrow, then we better start helping them do it today. We can teach what the school system wants us to teach in the ways that are best for our students.

"That's what I want—but where's the support?" In the end, it comes down to this. We can <u>say</u> all we want about doing things differently. We have to <u>show</u> people we mean it—not just through words, but in practice. Teachers want to make changes, but they need to feel supported. Let's think about what we can do. . . .

Principal Moseley looked down at their notes. "A little support for *ourselves* wouldn't hurt," he said, district office in mind.

Ms. Melder perked up. She didn't like where this was heading. But she hadn't stayed cozy, unbothered, and comfortable for as long as she had for no reason at all. Developing a fitness for achieving her ends, and for eliminating anything that stood in the way, was a skill she'd developed over time and with practice. By then, Ms. Melder was an oiled machine.

She agreed with the principal, but in the worst way. "It *is* about time we get the district involved . . ." she responded. Her meaning was clear.

"*Teachers are scared*," Ms. Melder said slowly. "They're worried about test scores—and why wouldn't they be? We all know the school's situation," she whispered, filling the room with an ominous air. "All the board needs now is one little reason . . . and 'poof'!" She snapped—and Jack jumped in his seat. "At the drop of a hat . . . Clover could vanish."

She made for the door. Then, turning, she told them, "Somebody needs to look out for our kids."

She opened the door, and then walked from the room.

Ms. Monica looked like she'd just seen a ghost. Two words sounded over and over in her head as she sat there, silently shaking.

"*Not now. . . .*"

The launch of the network was one week away.

PHASE 4: PLOT YOUR POSITION
Where are we now?

You won't know how to get where you're trying to go without first understanding where you already are.

When it comes down to where your school's currently positioned, a lot's likely good—and a lot's likely troubling. Luckily, it's not about where you are now. It's about where you're going together.

STEP 1. Reflect.

With your team, reflect on the journey of the Change Team at Clover, and discuss the discoveries they've made on the way. How have their experiences compared to your own, and what have you gathered from their journey together?

STEP 2. Dissect.

Access the **Cultural Well-Being Rubric** at www.depthvaledetectives.com. One at a time, dive deeply into each of the measure's dimensions (self-understanding, knowledge, competency, and connection). Then, discuss your findings with your team. What do you see? Are these outcomes now clearer in the context of school?

STEP 3. *Measure.*

Using the Cultural Well-Being Rubric, first individually and then as a team, measure where you are right now as a school. What evidence are you using to determine your ratings?

Discuss your findings as a team. What are you already doing that's good? Where's the most room for growth? What objections to contributive learning have been raised? Is yours a culture of instruction, or learning—of boundaries, or belonging—of crisis, or contribution?

STEP 4. *Design.*

Drawing on areas identified for growth, discuss what you can do *right now* for your students. How will you respond to the objections being raised? Identify concrete steps you can take to progress on the Cultural Well-Being Rubric.

ACTION.

See your school in the light of contributive learning. Where does that light shine the clearest and brightest, and where is it hard to make out? Pay mindful attention to the state of your school, and do what you can to cast light where it's needed.

COMING TO YOU LIVE

In the staff room at Clover on the day of the launch, teachers had gathered to live stream the show. And while Jack got the screen up and running for the watch party, four of them huddled in the back of the room.

"Check this out . . ." said Sam, a 2nd grade teacher, grinning as he pulled a piece of paper from his pocket. "I was feeling inspired at the staff meeting yesterday."

He handed the paper to a teacher standing next to him. She took a quick look, and then burst into laughter.

After the others had each done the same, one of them crinkled it into a ball, tossed it aside to the corner of the room, and rejoined the rest of the staff with the others.

Just then, from the office in the back of the staff room, Ms. Melder walked in—and went straight for the paper. She opened it slowly . . . then it fell to the floor.

With soft steps she walked from the staff room in silence.

In the doorway, Kaia stood patiently waiting as Jack finished prepping the room for the watch. She had come by to grab him for one final tech check . . . and witnessed the drama unfold.

Kaia walked quietly into the staff room and picked up the crinkled piece of paper off the floor. On it was a drawing depicting Ms. Melder. She was scowling—and dressed up as Crisis.

"All ready!" Jack said, calling out to Kaia, who still held the crinkled-up picture in her hand.

She dropped it in the trash and followed Jack from the room.

✳ ✳ ✳

"Ten . . . nine . . . eight . . . seven . . . six . . . five . . . four. . . ."

Kaia finished the countdown with only her fingers, silently queuing the anchors at zero. "*Go time . . .*" she whispered. And they were away.

"Hello and welcome to CloverTV, coming to you live from Clover K-8 School. I'm Jamie."

"And I'm Dylan," her co-anchor smiled. "And *this* . . . is Clover School News.

"As a network," said Dylan, "our purpose is simple. We want to tell stories that add to your lives."

"We want to contribute," Jamie picked up. "We're young . . . but it's never too early to add."

She paused momentarily. "And now, our first story."

With Jack's patient guidance (and some generous donations), the team built a studio—green screen and all. And so, when Jamie introduced their first story, its title flashed boldly behind the lead anchors.

"Recently," Jamie started, "we uncovered a problem. As students, we want more than good grades and test scores. We all want fulfilling and meaningful lives. *That's* why we learn," Jamie continued. "*We learn so that we contribute back*—we learn to make lives and communities better."

"And that's what we want school to look like," said Dylan. "Until it looks out for our well-being first, we'll *all* feel the weight of the Great Education Crisis."

That was the queue—and the team rolled the video.

In the weeks that had passed, the News Team worked tirelessly filming and interviewing a variety of people. From Kaia, Lucas, Jamie, and Dylan to Cameron, Wallace, and members of the Change Team, each made a case for contributive learning. And the video's message came through loud and clear:

Schools are positioned to prevent and solve crises, but right now they aren't doing nearly enough. It's a problem that makes a lot of people's lives hard. It's real, it's urgent—and here's how to solve it.

A few minutes into the video, Lucas said, "*The world needs more people who can stand up to Crisis . . . and that's why the world needs the Depthvale Detectives.*"

At that, the screen slowly faded to black. Then, softly at first, but then louder and louder, theme music (courtesy of Mr. B.'s Music Team) kicked off the first episode of *The Depthvale Detectives.*

Lucas's heart pounded out of his chest.

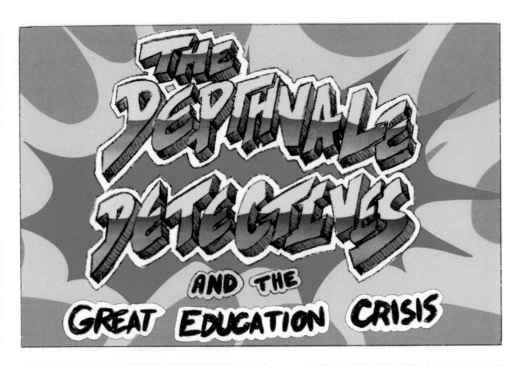

The villain behind all their struggles was Crisis. He hung around schools and made students' lives hard.

And the students could feel it, too. They saw what Crisis did to the world, and they knew that he had to be stopped.

Watching alone in her dark, empty classroom, Ms. Melder saw Crisis appear on the screen.

"If that's what they want . . . *then that's what they'll get.*"

Determined, she walked from the room.

Passing her colleagues in the staff room together, she turned left and walked toward the school's corner exit. There, by the little red box on the wall, she reached out her hand—and pulled down the handle.

CAUSE FOR ALARM

Ms. Monica's phone rang inside her apartment. The call was from Principal Moseley.

"Turn on Channel 9 . . ." he said. And she did.

Her phone nearly fell—Ms. Melder appeared.

"*The kids seem to feel pretty strongly . . .*" said the interviewer. "*So, what do you make of all this?*"

"Look," said Ms. Melder. "*The idea is cute. . . . But, in the end, kids don't know what's best. If we don't get back to the way things have been, what happens to them isn't going to be pretty. . . .*"

Ms. Monica curled herself into a ball.

On the other side of town, Kaia did, too. Soft little tears made their way from her eyes as she watched with her family on Channel 9 News.

But it wasn't from anger, or fear, or self-pity. Since the day of the launch, she felt for Ms. Melder.

∗　∗　∗

The interview aired the day after the launch. The next day was Friday.

Around 11:00 a.m., two unannounced visitors met with Principal Moseley—Sara, the superintendent of the district, and Bill, the longstanding president of the school board.

"*What are we going to do about this?* . . ." were among the first words Bill directed at the principal.

Sara had tried to talk the president down. But bad press and budget cuts, on top of Clover's "shortcomings," cleared out the path he was already following. And he didn't hold back on poor Principal Moseley.

At the end of the hour-long "discussion" that followed, Bill none-too-calmly delivered the verdict. He told Principal Moseley he'd land on his feet, that the students, of course, would be much better off—but that, at the close of the academic year, Clover would cease to exist.

When Ms. Monica checked on him later that day, Principal Moseley had his head in his hands. And back in the Depthvale Detectives' HQ, when Kaia checked in on the state of affairs Ms. Monica started to cry.

"I'm sorry, Kaia . . ." was all she could say.

A LITTLE CONNECTION

Jasmine could tell that her daughter was down.

"Hey . . ." she said as she stroked Kaia's hair, "why don't you visit your grandpa this weekend? You still haven't taken him up on his offer. . . ."

It took some convincing, but she said she would go.

Arriving at the nursing home early Sunday morning, Kaia walked up to her grandfather's room. She hugged him and asked, "How are you today?"

"Kaia," he said—she knew his answer by heart: "today is the greatest day of my life."

He studied his granddaughter. "Hmm . . . what's wrong?"

Sighing, she looked from the floor to her grandpa. "There are so many things to be down about, Grandpa. How are you always so 'up' on the world?"

He smiled. "There are two types of people, Kaia. Those who bring people down, and those who lift people up. If we're *up* on the world . . . we can lift other people."

He tenderly pressed Kaia's hands in his own. "Don't give up on anyone, or on doing what's right."

She smiled at her grandpa, and he laughed in reply. "Are you ready?" he asked her. "Your audience awaits. . . ."

In the nursing home's daycare a few minutes later, Kaia sat down before old folks and young ones and read them the story of the Depthvale Detectives.

While reading, she looked at those gathered around her—the elderly and all they'd experienced in their lives, and the kids and their futures and the world they'd grow up in. She hoped it was a world where they all felt belonging, and where they got what they needed to lift people up.

She knew what was right. And she wouldn't give up.

* * *

The Mission Log of the Depthvale Detectives

Mission: Lift-Up
Target Code Name: Queen Contribution
Tools: Self-Understanding ✔ Knowledge ✔ Competency ✔
Connection ✔
Objective: Belonging.
Priority: 1

Time Log:
Monday, 9:01 a.m.: Kaia calls for a meeting of the Depthvale Detectives in the Depthvale Detectives' HQ.

Tuesday, 2:00 p.m.: The Detectives commence a team brainstorming session that lasts through the end of the school day.

Wednesday, 3:17 p.m.: Kaia, Lucas, Jamie, and Dylan walk into Lucas's house.

Thursday, 4:43 p.m.: Ms. Monica enters a dark, empty classroom and places a large, purple envelope on the desk.

Friday, 3:30 p.m.: The "CloverTV Community Celebration" begins in the Clover gymnasium.

The mysterious fire alarm may have cut the launch short, but the students didn't see it as a reason not to celebrate. In fact, it gave them *more* reason to celebrate—now, they could broadcast the rest of their show.

So, they invited their families and friends, all Clover's staff, even Sara and Bill . . . to a short celebration of CloverTV.

Some of the attendees shared words at the microphone, and they screened a recording of "The Great Education Crisis" (making Bill more than a little uncomfortable). And at the moment the news story came to a close, the students sat proudly with families and friends as the audience melted in rapturous cheers.

But, at that very same jubilant moment . . . nobody noticed Ms. Melder take the stage.

"*Ahem. . . .*"

Ms. Melder cleared her throat into the microphone. The crowd fell eerily silent. Principal Moseley and Ms. Monica were stunned. Their looks spoke the same helpless cry: "*Oh, no. . . .*"

Ms. Melder held all of their fates in her hands.

"Before we live 'happily ever after,'" she mocked, "there's something you all need to hear."

She waited. The audience moved to the edge of their seats.

"I've opposed all this nonsense from the very beginning, saying over and over, 'It isn't going to work.' And I said it for one simple reason." She paused. "*I didn't want it to work.*"

At that, she suddenly softened her features.

"I wanted to *keep doing* what I'd *been doing* . . ." she said, "to look out for me . . . to just stay the same. . . .

"Well," she continued, "it just wasn't working. I was putting my interests ahead of my students'. I had my way—they needed another. I *pushed* my students to learn what they needed—I should have been *pulling* them closer to me. I rejected my colleagues—I should have connected."

She looked at the rest of the Change Team and smiled. "Luckily, it's never too late to begin. So, to my colleagues, my students, and your families . . . *I want this to work*—so let's make it happen."

The cheers that erupted were the loudest of the night. Students and teachers stood up and applauded, and Ms. Melder, clutching a large, purple envelope, practically floated her way off the stage.

Still in his seat, Bill nearly fainted. He and Ms. Melder had been in cahoots—he hadn't expected this turn for the worse.

Bill whispered to Sara, "If she wants to go down with the ship then so be it. This doesn't change Clover's situation in the least."

But Sara was no longer sitting beside him. She walked up to Principal Moseley in the crowd. "If there's anything you need," she said, "let me know."

Principal Moseley gave Sara his thanks. "*There's hope left for Clover,*" he thought to himself.

A few minutes later, Bill met Sara in the parking lot.

"You're making a horrible mistake," he said coldly, telling Sara again that, in the story of Clover, an unhappy ending was still in the cards.

But Sara's eyes flashed back at Bill in defiance. "If you're taking down Clover . . . then take me down, too."

Bill told her he would.

But the evening told otherwise. In the gym, the students and families still gathered, none of them wanting the evening to end.

Eventually, Kaia parted ways with her friends and rejoined her parents, brother, and grandpa.

"The long reign of Crisis has ended," said Wallace, as they all cast affectionate smiles at Kaia.

"Long live Contribution!" she beamed in reply.

They wandered out happily into the night.

A COMMITMENT TO CONTRIBUTION

When fall rolled around and the leaves started changing, Clover's doors opened as planned for the school year.

In fact, they never even closed for the summer. "Clover School News doesn't take summer break!" Dylan said in the spring. And his News Team agreed.

They worked through the summer and recorded in studio—thanks, in large part, to the adult volunteer team, headlined by Cameron, Jack, and Ms. Monica. And they didn't have any more problems with fire alarms. . . .

First chance he got, Sam apologized for the picture. But Ms. Melder didn't hold any grudges against him.

"Your picture was spot on!" she said, laughing warmly. "I *was* like Crisis . . . but I'm ready for a change. It's time for less Crisis and more Contribution."

For the rest of the year (and forever thereafter), Ms. Melder kept the contents of that large, purple envelope pinned to a prominent place on her wall—except for, of course, when she read it to her students.

THE DEPTHVALE DETECTIVES

AND

QUEEN CONTRIBUTION

BY MS. MONICA'S CLASS

Slowly but surely, the Depthvale community got back on its feet.

Lucas's mom found a job that she loved, and Channel 9 News tried to get Wallace back. But he politely declined. An old passion reemerged . . . and he started teaching journalism at Depthvale High School. And when a community partner commissioned a mural on the wall of a building beside Clover's playground, Clover knew Jasmine was up to the task.

It hadn't come easy for Cameron—far from it. But with the past year's experience, he knew what to do. And not wanting to wander too far from his family, he enrolled in the film school at a nearby university.

The students had big plans for CloverTV. By then, the News Team made "newsing" look easy. Jamie and Dylan still shined as lead anchors, and Kaia's production was a sight to behold. Mason reported on everything sports, and Tori had started a segment of her own. She picked out some content off Clover's social media to feature on episodes of "Talking with Tori."

And Lucas's number one goal for the fall? Adding animation to *The Depthvale Detectives*. Needless to say, he was well on his way.

Other students got in on the action, too, and it wasn't just those in Ms. Monica's classroom. Some helped with shows, some started their own, and others helped out with *The Clover Contributor*—a new site committed to everything Clover. In one of the website's most popular features, students could share all about who they were, what they were learning, and all they contribute. It was open to anyone, of all grades and ages, and fittingly titled "In Clover."

Of course, it was hard moving on from Ms. Monica. The students missed hearing her voice every day, and they often thought back on their time the past year.

But it wasn't like they didn't get to see her anymore. In fact, they still got to see her a lot. She was there for the students whenever they needed her, and she and Jack were still active with CloverTV.

So, in time, they saw the change differently. "We're expanding the Depthvale Detectives' HQ!" Now, HQ wasn't only one classroom— it spread across every last corner of Clover.

Besides, they all loved their new teacher, too, who greeted them warmly on the first day of school.

"Welcome, Detectives!" said a kind, caring voice. "Have you all come back ready to contribute this year?"

The students all smiled and assured her they did. They could tell that they'd get along fine with Ms. Melder.

*   *   *

Despite having earned Sara's willing support (and the unwilling exit of the old school board president), Clover still met with a number of critics—people with a penchant for staying the same—who told them:

"Your students won't be here forever. They'll leave you behind for high school and college, then to enter the workforce and get on with their lives. Their new schools will have more traditional focuses, and you can bet their employers have other concerns. . . .

"Sooner or later, no matter what you do here, your students will have to come back to reality. And reality's sure to hit hard."

But the people at Clover knew better than that. "Wherever they go when they leave us," they answered, "our students will make it a better place."

At Clover, that's what they learned how to do.

When the Change Team started planning for the school year ahead, Principal Moseley shared a wealth of ideas—one, a new Student Change Team at Clover. So, when it launched at the start of the year, Kaia, Lucas, and other young leaders saw to it that all students' voices were heard. And Ms. Monica and Ms. Melder, the team's teacher leaders, made sure the two Change Teams worked closely together.

And Principal Moseley had other plans, too. He invited some parents and members of the community to join with the Change Team's "original six," as a proud Mr. B. liked to call them.

And Mrs. McCarthy loved every last minute. "I feel like I'm twenty again!" she exclaimed. The rest of the Change Team was feeling it, too.

"Well, team," said Principal Moseley, "I don't know about you, but I think we're ready." The rest of the Change Team wholeheartedly agreed. They had come a long way—it was time to commit.

PHASE 5: COMMIT TO CONTRIBUTION

It started as a simple idea in the Change Team, but quickly spread out through the Clover community. All sorts of partners shared valuable input, and the Change Team in the end put their thoughts to the page.

From then on, it hung on the wall by the entrance, signed by each member of Clover's school staff and with space for the signatures of students and parents and anyone else who was ready to commit.

It challenged the Clover community daily to honor their commitment to contributive learning.

CL🍀VER SCHOOL
COMMITMENT TO CONTRIBUTION

OUR PURPOSE IS CONTRIBUTION.

SO, WE WILL DEVELOP SELF–UNDERSTANDING.

WE WILL CULTIVATE KNOWLEDGE OF THE WORLD AND ITS WORKINGS.

WE WILL FOSTER THE COMPETENCY TO USE WHAT WE LEARN.

WE WILL MAKE CONNECTIONS WITH OTHERS AND THE WORLD.

WE WILL NOT BRING DOWN—WE WILL LIFT PEOPLE UP.

WE WILL NOT SUBTRACT—WE WILL ADD TO THE WORLD.

WE WILL STAND UP TO CRISIS, EVERY DAY, WITH CONTRIBUTION.

WE LEARN SO THAT WE CONTRIBUTE BACK.

＊　＊　＊

Kaia walked through the entrance of Clover K-8 School and stopped for a read of the school's new Commitment.

She smiled, thinking back on their journey so far, and slowly spoke Clover's new motto out loud. *"We learn so that we contribute back."*

She signed, then hurried off after her classmates.

A new year was starting, and they had so much to add.

PHASE 5: COMMIT TO CONTRIBUTION
Are we ready to commit?

With the self-understanding, knowledge, competency, and connections developed in your time as a Change Team, the time's come to ask the big question together:

Are we ready to commit to contributive learning?

STEP 1. Reflect.

With your team, reflect on the story you read. Which characters and events have stuck with you, and why? What have they helped you to learn about learning, your school, yourself, your students, and others?

Then, reflect on the story you *lived*. What's the story of your school since you formed a Change Team? Reflect on your journey, and describe your experience.

STEP 2. Discuss.

Take time to discuss the commitment. What does it mean to commit to contribution? What will it take from the Change Team, the school, the students, the parents, and the rest of the community? Remember, you don't have to wait 'til you're *there*— this is a commitment to getting there, together.

Share final thoughts, reflections, and feelings—with honesty, openness, mindfulness, and belonging.

STEP 3. Commit.

Are we ready to commit to contributive learning—to ourselves, one another, and *all* of our students?

If the answer is "yes," then you know what to do.

ACTION.

Develop self-understanding.
Cultivate knowledge.
Foster competency.
Make connections.

Don't bring down—lift people up.
Don't subtract—add to the world.

Stand up to crisis, every day, with contribution.

THE END.

* * *

THE AUTHORS

Joanne McEachen, Founder and CEO of The Learner First, brings over 30 years of experience to offer insights and strategies that change the lives of students and educators. A leading voice in the global education community, Joanne's insights are illuminated by continued, hands-on experience with groups from different cultures, backgrounds, and schools around the world. She has published several books on teaching, learning, and system change, and also serves as a founding Executive of Karanga: The Global Alliance for Social Emotional Learning and Life Skills.

Matthew Kane works closely with school communities to improve students' outcomes and share learning stories. A Director at The Learner First, Matthew has partnered with diverse schools and school systems globally to develop contributive learning tools, language, and practices. He coauthored *Measuring Human Return: Understand and Assess What Really Matters for Deeper Learning* and graduated from the University of Notre Dame.

Made in the USA
Coppell, TX
01 September 2020

35787682R10083